These are clear eyed poems, carefully, beautifully, constructed and informed by years of being in communion with homeless folks who share with the attentive writer, then caring soup kitchen director, "The things we cannot name are splinters growing slowly toward skin." Ruth Dickey uses form and content to great effect reminding us that we are all fallible and flawed, that we are all in search for "The comfort of what is familiar," and more importantly, that not one of us "gets to wear a white hat."

—*Claudia Castro Luna*
Washington State Poet Laureate

In Ruth Dickey's *Mud Blooms* a world builds around us from everything we neglected to admire: a starfish's "unfurling arms, anemone undulating," the "bathing...[of] shoeless, cracking feet," or "the frenzy of petals." Dickey shines a light both on the beauty of the everyday and on the extraordinary, placing them on equal ground. With the patience for beauty of an origami artist, Dickey takes time to develop the shape of her scenes and the music of her lines. She's a poet with the rare gift not only of the line that sings but also of a song that bears truth. Now, because I trust both her and her poems, reading *Mud Blooms*, "I understand this is the purest form of comfort."

—*A. Van Jordan*
Author of Rise, PEN/Oakland Josephine Miles Award, Guggenheim Fellow

In an age of social and political divisiveness, Ruth Dickey's poems of loss, hunger and survival are not only vital but necessary. In her debut, *Mud Blooms*, the poet deftly weaves together three stories: reckoning with her mother's "winding down" from age and illness, working at Miriam's Kitchen with a menagerie of sympathetic and unruly characters, and her travels and discoveries in Latin America. In her capable hands, people who might have been portrayed as maudlin or pandered to are made real; she has given a voice to the vulnerable and overlooked and they are feisty, complicated, dirty, poetic and deserving of love. Like all of us. Her masterful poem "Alphabet Soup Kitchen" is told with a journalist's eye for detail and a straightforward wit and self awareness. This is not poetry as charity; Dickey sets a table and makes sure there's a seat for everyone. In moments of vulnerability, the language of the poems rise to the level of prayers. In *Mud Blooms*, Ruth Dickey has crafted a road map that leads back to our very own humanity.

—*Sjohnna McCray*
Author of Rapture, winner of the Walt Whitman Award

Ruth Dickey's poems are a fusion of lyrical narration and inventive imagery grounded in grief and loss that she forever overcomes through her poetic insights and affirmations.

—*Jack Hirschman*
Poet Laureate of San Francisco

mud blooms

mud blooms

RUTH DICKEY

Harbor Mountain Press
White River Junction, Vermont

ISBN 978-0-9882755-7-7

Harbor Mountain Press is a non-profit press publishing books of high literary merit. For more information, or to donate to the press, please go to harbormountainpress.org

Harbor Mountain Press books are distributed by Small Press Distribution in Berkeley, California; for orders and more information about our titles, please go to spdbooks.org

Series Editor: Peter Money
MURA Award & Projects Manager: Lenore DeCerce
Design: Andrew Miller-Brown
Cover Painting: *Float*, 2017 © Sarah Lutz
MURA Award Advisors: Michelle Ollie & Partridge Boswell

Acknowledgments

The titles of the poems that appear in *italics* in this collection are lines from poems written by homeless and formerly homeless writers who participated in writing workshops I founded and led at Miriam's Kitchen in Washington, DC (1994-2002). All of the lines cited appeared in either *167 Wednesdays*, *167 Thursdays*, or *Soft Concrete Stairs*, two collections of artwork and writing from the workshops published by Miriam's Kitchen in 1997 and 2002 respectively. Many thanks to all of the writers with whom I had the honor of working, and particular thanks to the writers whose lines appear as poem titles in this order:

Laverne Worrell

Patricia Freeman

Andrew Applewhait

Fernando Figueroa

DE Taylor

Paul Franey

James Mann

Patricia Freeman

David Harris

Vsbyara

Neal Avery

Stephanie Green

Lee Levy

Neal Avery

DE Taylor

Andrew Applewhait

Larry Kyle

David Harris

Larry Mitchell

Joseph Wise

Ricky Balthrop

Larry Heelen

My deepest thanks also go to the following journals where versions of the following poems appeared:

Alimentum, "Alphabet Soup Kitchen," nominated for a Pushcart
The American Journal of Poetry, "*no one gets to wear a white hat*," "*I think I'm getting the Christmas spirit*," "The letters, 1," "*Of broken folk*," and "*Take deep breaths/ hold a pen/ sit still*."
The Baltimore Review, "*What Robin Hood Really Did*,"
Barrow Street, "San Cristobal de las Casas: Three Sonnets,"
Cincinnati Review, "In my wallet,"
Divide, "Somoto, Nicaragua #2,"
Ellipsis, "*Luck is My Myth for Blessing*,"
HazMat Review, "*The mundane problems of self preservation are constantly on every mind*,"

Kalliope, "San Jose, Costa Rica,"
Ocean City Review, "Wilmington, NC," and "The Letters, 2,"
Paper Street, "*Not enough dimes or cents or styrofoam cups. Not
      enough streetcorners.*" "Somoto, Nicaragua #1,"
Potomac Review, "*Everything Dodges Away*,"
Roger, "Estate Sale,"
Slant, "Finding Greenway Esmont on my birthday"
Slipstream, "*Life Didn't Cease to Be*,"
Sonora Review, "*He Smoke to Make the Night Go Long*," and "*What
      they become when you were not*,"
Sycamore Review, "Somoto, Nicaragua #3,"
Zocalo Public Square, "Carolina Clay"

20 of the poems titled with lines from the Miriam's Kitchen Poets
also appeared in the chapbook, *Paper Houses, Sky Ceiling* (Pudding
House Press, 2006).

I am profoundly grateful to the DC Commission on the Arts and
Humanities with funding from the National Endowment for the
Arts whose support helped make this work possible.

Contents

Making up names for the regulars

Somoto, Nicaragua #3   3

87 days after she found a lump   4

Four-twenty-one   5

He Smoke to Make the Night go Long   6

What they become when you were not   7

Alphabet Soup Kitchen: a, b, c, d   8

About the hungers coming

Apple Cake   13

Somoto, Nicaragua #1   14

Wilmington, NC   15

What Robin Hood Really Did   16

The rain fell with open care

   like flowers blooming alone for the groom   17

Memories become more important than dreams   18

e, f, g, h   19

Open palms, smeared with mud

origami boat   23

Estate Sale   24

Mercado, San Cristobal de las Casas: Three Sonnets   25

no one gets to wear a white hat   26

Not enough dimes or cents or styrofoam cups.

   Not enough street corners.   28

Luck is my myth for blessing   29

Each life must have an intermission   30

i, j, k   31

Warm tents we inhabit

Barbeque   35
Mantequilla de Maní   37
Somoto, Nicaragua #2   38
The alkalis and nitrates of your sacred offerings   39
Life didn't cease to be   40
Where are you going to show your light today?   41
l, m, n   43

Holding gravity

Over and over I get the idea   45
In my wallet   46
I think I'm getting the Christmas spirit   47
This night will go on for days to come   48
She yellow teenage whorehouse   49
Grip the steeple bravely with your toes   50
The last days are with us, a lost poem   51
o, p, q, r   52

Day by day, my holes get bigger

brown shirt   55
Finding Greenway Esmont on my birthday   56
The letters, 1   58
Of broken folk   60
I learned to be scared at an early age   61
The mundane problems of self preservation
        are constantly on every mind   62
s, t, u, v   64

Carry me to morning

w, x, y, z	67
Everything dodges away	69
San Jose, Costa Rica	70
Carolina Clay	71
The letters, 2	72
Ecola State Park	74
Take deep breaths/ hold a pen/ sit still	75

for the Miriam's Kitchen Poets
and all of us searching for home

Making up names for the regulars

Somoto, Nicaragua, #3

Dona Ophe entrusted me with the key to the orphanage's supply room,
dark with sunlight filtering in bright strips,

snowstorms of dust above boards worn shiny by bare feet.
Amidst old blankets, a sack of beans, spider webs,

disguised by ordinary burlap it sat: a sack of sugar,
not refined white that fills bowls at home, but thick grains brown

like sand, crystals fat as sea salt. My assignment was to bring one cup
for a refresco from green lemons the younger girls pulled from a tree.

And yet, I lingered in the room, watched dust circling, inserted first one
dampened finger, pulled grains to my lips. Just beans every meal, no corn

for tortillas, no rice, portions shrinking every day. I had never known
hunger till then: the sharp shame of inserting a whole hand,

raising clutched fingers to my lips, secrecy of the hushed storage room,
my own shrill needs that humbled me to taste, crystal by fistful.

Hunger pushed the taste beyond sweet to sharp. I hated
my desire, pure as thirst, simple as lemons.

I don't remember leaving the room, remember only vaguely
the refresco, beans that followed, though still I am haunted

by the slanting light, the feel of my fingers grasping.
Now when I pour spoonfuls in my coffee, they bring

the smell of cooking fires, songs the girls taught me, carrying
small ones in my arms to swing on mango trees, older ones

picking lice from my hair. Rough rotting boards, old mango trees,
forgive us our hungers, forgive me my stolen grains.

87 days after she found a lump

I am washing my mother's incision,
jagged badge of bunched purple red ribbon

across her heart. Our bathroom expands to fill
the entire world: slow drip of faucets

purple of bruise, yellow of healing,
brown of dried blood. My focus

is a Moebius strip; if I can just
get this right, cleanse and rebandage,

I can right the indignity of the surgeon's knife.
I know it's silly, and I focus anyway,

feeling each tug of the washcloth
will make amends or make things worse.

After, I wash her hair gingerly
knowing, soon she'll have no hair to wash.

The water spirals down the drain
and my mom murmurs *It will be all right;*

the world is no larger or smaller than this:
these apple-scented bubbles, this stream of warm water

our hope, this scar, these hands.

Four-twenty-one

Our parents wouldn't let us name him, so we called him
421, from the yellow tag stapled to the black fur of his left ear.

More dog than calf, he liked to lick the salt
from our skin, followed us beneath the grape arbor,

through clover patches, back to the chicken house
where he'd tickle corn from our bare hands.

I liked him because he followed us and hated blackberries,
toothy brambles and fat berries hiding too many

seeds. And though we couldn't name him, like the Toyota
we'd christened *Pearly*, the rabbit *Clover*, the persimmon tree

by the clothesline *Sam*, we sang him songs with his new name,
murmuring into his too-big eyes, the number growing

sweet and fat as he did, as the blackberrries, as the corn
when it sat in water. In a few weeks he outgrew

the chicken house, moved to our neighbors' pasture with George,
the mean old cow, who chased us if we came inside the barbed wire fence.

Six months and he was sold, the pasture only George.
The things we cannot name are splinters

working slowly out toward skin:
my blackberry stain memories of the pasture

with mean old George and piles of manure,
my brother and me leaning on the fence, stretching our hands through.

He Smoke to Make the Night go Long

he sits on wooden bench, not concrete
which holds the cold, gives arthritis

strikes each match against sidewalk
cups hands against wind distractions

waits for the truck that comes at six
mealy apple and soup congealing

wears seven watches to keep the hours
double socks and double pants

reads dictionaries to keep the words
smokes to make the night uncurl

What they become when you were not

They become ice-cream cones,
pimento cheese sandwiches,
become kittens and petticoats.

When you were not,
the world was small,
was dry toast, no lipstick.

They become paperclips, stamps,
dust in sun ray. Lonely they.
Quiet they. When you become

little girl, they yawn, come
calling. Little petticoat girl
with cone hat, strawberry eyes.

Nobody sees but you
dust in ears, kitten in lungs.
Before you, they were still.

Sing dust songs,
sandwich songs.
You special, you becoming

and they happy.
You sing to them, they sing
to only you, only you.

Alphabet Soup Kitchen: a, b, c, d

Apples are a terrible idea in soup kitchens. At Miriam's Kitchen, we served fruit slick with syrup. I figured fresh fruit tastes better than canned, so I started ordering apples because they are cheap. But if you have dental problems, it's really hard to eat apples. Almost everyone who is homeless has dental problems, because the only free dental care is pulled teeth. So everyone hated my apples. Junior told me only an idiot would order apples. The only way people ate apples was chopped up and mixed in canned fruit salad, which Junior loved.

Bob came to the weekly poetry workshop I ran after breakfast at the kitchen. My favorite poem of his was, "No More Streetlights in my House." After two years at the kitchen, I spent a year and half in New Orleans. One day in New Orleans, I got a call at work from Bob. If you are homeless, finding a place to make even a local call is like trying to get a free ride on Giuliani's New York subway. I was sure Bob was calling long distance to tell me someone had died. But Bob was delighted he had just received a letter saying his poem, "Streetlights," won a contest. He could purchase the anthology in which it appeared for only $39.95. *And I'm going to use the $5,000 prize money for a deposit and first month's rent!* Years later, Bob still turned up at the kitchen. I never asked about the money.

Christine's face was instantly recognizable on the missing person flyer sent by the National Alliance on Mental Illness. Her green eyes and tangled hair had been at breakfast almost every day for months. In the picture, she looked cleaner and softer. I called her sister, whose number was on the flyer; she sobbed. The sister had been looking for Christine for months. She said, *Everyone thinks I don't love her because she's on the street, but there's nothing I can do unless I can prove she's a danger to herself or others. She believes I'm trying to poison her and won't come home. Everyone thinks I'm a terrible sister. Do you?*

Down a set of concrete stairs, in the basement of a church, you can find Miriam's Kitchen. Fifteen round tables with red folding chairs. Walls covered with paintings by folks who eat breakfast there, like Bob and Donald. On one side are tables of cereal, juice, and milk/

sugar/coffee. Enter and get a number you will trade for your hot breakfast. Most people come every day, every day. Some come a few times a month. Others come once or twice and never come again.

About the hungers coming

Apple cake

Past the garden in the side yard, we had an apple orchard,
orchard perhaps an overstatement for five trees,

four of them small. Violets beneath the largest tree, so old
the branches touched the ground, spring canopy of snowy petals,

speckled mock strawberries' yellow blooms. Mostly the apples
rotted on the ground, buzzing with wasps; small, hard, too tart.

But some years apple sauce, and most years my favorite:
apple cake, baked in a deep bundt with a center post,

pan never used for other cakes, apples never so good as this:
crisp-edged crumb, gold of November sun, apple dappled

One year a woman with long dark hair and her little girl
came to ask if they could pick the apples, gathered

paper bags full, carried them away, and I was jealous.
Didn't want to share, even the rotting bounty. Even now

my miserly heart stings me, the yellowjacket somehow
in my bed. Like all the lost things, I crave apple cake

but never learned to make it, lost both pan and recipe.

Somoto, Nicaragua #1

Someone was shaking me. Heavy
with sleep, I knew only darkness, cot, moon, shaking.

As a child, I sucked my thumb till seven, till I was bribed
to stop, and now in sleep I sucked words,

dreaming of the ugliness of English,
its nasal twangs and awkward stops, the rrr's

like barking dogs, hungering for language's
faded flannel to stop my shaking.

Suyapa stood by my cot, her bare feet gray in moonlight
shaking my shoulder. I don't know what she said,

but I twisted the words to English, heard *Are you okay?*
This was impossible, but I smiled, my relief

palpable; we never question things we want badly enough.
Que dijiste? What did you say? I saw words

I longed to take into my mouth: *home, hope, hold*
the o's stretching and moving to *yo*, to endings marking

first person present, to *ahora y como*, for *now* and *how*.
She shook her head, pulled her thumb from her mouth.

Tuve una pesadilla, I had a nightmare. I stroked her hair,
gray in moonlight, tucked her back

into her cot, sang softly, first in English and then
in Spanish, songs the girls taught me playing school,

confirming Suyapa as good teacher, me as good student,
our mouths full of moon and song and breath.

Wilmington, NC

Fleeing beeps and whorls, passing minutes till sunrise,
I snuck out of the hospital to smoke on the granite steps,

the night damp, giant moon hanging, a tin ornament
behind magnolias. Grateful reprieve from vinyl chair,

from curling on the laminate arm, waking to the pulse ox alarm,
nurse rounds, yawning chasm of hours, mom squirming on her back,

more infant than parent, everything unspooling.

I keep coming back to this night. The yellow of the moon.
Bitter coffee in a styrofoam cup. Something languid in the air,

Spanish moss like swaying kelp. Horrible yes, but also
oddly open, a starfish unfurling arms, anemone undulating.

What Robin Hood Really Did

All y'all supposed to be helping, supposed to get a man
on his feet: just fat ticks on a mangy dog.

Without me, you'd be out of work. You'd be Monopoly money.
Same as the jail lets a man out in a t-shirt, no coat in January.

Want a man hungry enough to get locked back up.
And you, you want a man on the street. You want

a man in here every day so you can feel good.
Nobody asked if I want your damn eggs. Don't think

I don't know. You keep me down, picture me hungry and you
handing me something. Hold that picture like some lucky penny

you found. What's it take to run this place? Three hundred grand?
Hundred and fifty people sitting in here hungry. You do the math.

Two grand a piece. Security deposit, first month's rent.
New clothes, food that I picked. Stop keeping a man down.

You want to help me, you got to give up what you got.

The rain fell with open care
　　like flowers blooming alone for the groom

For me, for me alone,
flowers bloom, exhale arias.
The simpering dresses I watch,

arranged on granite church steps,
are deaf. Silly frills think holding
means possession. From my bench

of cracking wood, I watch,
I know: each petal opens
to embrace me. Pigeons gather,

my flock of groomsmen; I call
and disperse the hopping rats.
I, pied piper of beauty.

Naïve bride emerges. Believes
the bouquet is hers,
hers to hold and hers to toss

to waiting crowds she imagines
clap for her. I am smarter than silly girls
in white. She is showered

in rice, while raindrops bloom only for me,
kissing each hair on my head,
bathing my shoeless, cracking feet.

I point at trees and they become
a frenzy of petals. I demand tulips,
crocuses from dirt, hear *I do* from dandelions.

Memories become more important than dreams

My balustrades are all behind me. I was
an architect, crafted cupolas, framed views.
Sent suits to the drycleaner. Had Palladian
windows, a garlic press. Meat for dinner
every night. Toasted champagne
in Corinthian flutes. Served the Navy,
saw Germany and Paris and Vietnam.
I know the latitude of Guam.

When I can't sleep, I walk each room
of what was once mine. Caress each cornice.
Brush fingers over drycleaning bags,
thin like clinging dreams. Hide my toes
in thick acrylic pile. Stroke porcelain cisterns:
sink, bathtub, toilet. Trace cool casings,
return to doorknobs that wait behind. Pass palms
over drywall, linger at light switches.

Perhaps I'll die like Gaudi in the midst
of building Sagrada Família, guts gushing
in the street because no taxi driver believes
the things I've built. But these nights, I make circuits
of each cantilevered corner, repeating steps,
savoring mental tromp l'oeil, building
a charge to warm fingers and toes,
to carry me to morning.

e, f, g, h

Eggs were for breakfast every Monday and Wednesday. Lines always longer on egg days. 95 people on Tuesday, 145 on Wednesday. We usually scrambled the eggs. Add a capful of vinegar to raw eggs or they'll turn green in aluminum serving pans. Sometimes we added chopped tomatoes, ham, or green peppers, but always only to half. Some people get very upset if you put things in their eggs.

Frank was a junkie. I should have known because he always wore long sleeves, even in summer, to hide the track marks. His hands were dry and cracked, his shaking fingers yellowed. I hired him to help clean. He was always willing to unload heavy cases of orange juice from the van or sweep the stairs. Frank frequently disappeared a day or two, but eventually he just stopped coming. Rumor was he had cancer and died. But you can't believe everything you hear. One day we were smoking outside, and he said, *I'd like to find the guy who gave me my first hit, and I'd like to kill him.*

George had too-bright eyes and liked to pump your hand up and down and up and down, to never let go. Six foot four, grass and leaves in his hair. One day, as I hurried to a meeting, George started walking with me. Talking nonsense; I wasn't really listening. Told him I was late, and he grabbed me. I screamed. No one stopped to help before I twisted away. When I called George's case manager to let him know, he told me George often grabs women when he's been drinking, and that I should set better boundaries. He said next time I should handle it better; next time I should call the police.

High-end food, liked smoked salmon, was not a big hit at our soup kitchen. We got leftovers from fancy parties, unwanted Christmas presents. A giant tray of salmon with capers and lemon wedges. Served it with eggs. The volunteers all drooled. Grandma, one of our sassier breakfast guests, asked, *What the hell is that?*

Open palms, smeared with mud

origami boat

I don't remember if it was my dad's idea first, or my brother's
or mine, but one of us decided we should make an origami

boat. Not a small one we could fit in our palms, or glide amidst
the salt and pepper shakers, saccharine tablets for buoys,

but a giant one, large enough we could sail
the aboveground pool in our backyard. We began

with newspapers, layers and layers we shellacked, building.
Once sheets were large enough, dad folded, an acrobatic feat

we never questioned, sure he could set the moon
next to our butter dish, leash an amoeba for a stroll. We

enveloped it with more shellac, smeared newsprint glowing
crystalline and sturdy. At last seaworthy, we carried

to the backyard. I remember evening and cold,
the first star just appearing above the persimmon tree, the sky

releasing its final tangerine stripes. We lowered the boat, and I
stepped one foot in, puncturing the floor, filling with water.

Our disappointment hung, a cloud of mosquitoes. And though we
devised plans for how to fold a better boat, chicken wire

between layers, we never built it. The pool became a hatchery
for tree frogs for two summers, filling each night with barking song.

Estate Sale

I ache for the 1946 Grimsley High School yearbook
resting beside a child's set of *Encyclopedia Britannica*,
the box of alphabetized records and dance cards,

photo albums spilling from a ripped box,
each fading caption: *Aunt Mavis, Uncle Jim*.
Even more painful, photos with no names at all.

Folding tables sag with porcelain birds,
candy dishes and chipped salt cellars;
an arc of furniture surrounds the house.

I can't stop wondering where the children are,
the ones who looked up goiters in the encyclopedia,
who learned each name, wrote thank-you notes

to Aunt Mavis and begged babysitters
to teach them to square dance. I avert my eyes
from these personal artifacts, strewn

like yellowed bras and boxers
across the lawn, while strangers poke and haggle.
The auctioneer spews a staccato rhythm

of numbers and possibilities; the crowd
jostles closer to see each proffered item.
Some have brought lawn chairs; a trailer

sells nachos. And yet, as I imagine
commandeering the microphone, stopping
these transactions, there is some small comfort

believing these things will find new homes, some
grain of relief imagining our lives amount to something
someone else might want, might name.

Mercado, San Cristobal de las Casas: Three Sonnets

you come with huge, upturned eyes   selling *chicle, plumas, pulceras*, shoe shines

Cómprame rings in my ears like a bell   calling me to a table where you are not invited

my friend buys tiny *chicles* in pastel colors   the thought of chewing makes me dizzy

I say no, over and over again   like a prayer

one day, in the market   you appear

my purchases weigh like hot stones   burn my hands as you ask

I relent and we walk to the pastry stand   *Cómprame uno. Regálame un peso.*

you select the moment's desire   and four more children appear, grinning

the vendor smiles   telling me the smallest one's favorite

Torta de piña   many people must do this

I could purchase her whole stand   coating the city

with sugar and flour   like an unexpected snowstorm

it would never be enough   the bell still rings

I buy placemats, napkins, haggling over pesos   my stomach fills with ash and stones

no one gets to wear a white hat

At four thirty the alarm shatters; I always forget
where I am, knowing only boiling
hurry. Wiping slime of sleep
from my eyes, I ride the white
fog of coffee and cigarettes through empty streets,
mind bustling with lists which grind

into cavities. Day begins measuring coffee grounds
carefully dividing. Outside, forgotten
fathers, brothers alight on corners, a mardi gras street
parade of ghosts in wool blankets carrying trash bags which boil
over with clothes, bedding, important white
papers turning slowly to papier mache. Some sleep,

heads on backpacks, elbows on sleeping
bags. A mustached man, still drunk, grinds
teeth rhythmically, matching can openers white
volunteers from the suburbs are scraping below, forgetting
to add vinegar to eggs as water boils
for grits. Sickly glow of street

lights is surpassed by hubbub of morning. Street
people shuffle with stories over coffee: *Last night was too cold to sleep.*
Cops made me move four times. Like a car crash, a woman throws boiling
water from the coffee machine down a man's back. Conversations grind
to a halt. She vanishes and returns the next morning, having forgotten
the incident. DC's men in white

coats tell me there is nothing they can do, and my off-white
organic cotton sheets gray and ensnare. Streets
cover my pillowcases, I forget
why I came here. I knew a man who beat another to death in his sleep
with a rock. I have seen a broke man give away his last cigarette. What grinds
most deeply are these sudden kindnesses, chiaroscuro against boiling

* * *

asphalt. It would be easier if these days were like hard-boiled
eggs, the center unthreateningly greenish-gray, the white
easy to separate. But we scramble our eggs, and the coffee grounds
snagged in my throat are the savage gentleness of dumpster diving, street
staccato of bucket drummers and high heels, cardboard castles for sleeping
under bridges, insomnia, my cloak to ward off what I struggle to remember and forget.

No sleep is deep enough to forget what a man with collapsing veins
and ground-up shoes whispered to me on a street
corner one boiling March morning: no one gets to wear a white hat.

Not enough dimes or cents or styrofoam cups.
  Not enough street corners.

Get your own damn corner. This one's mine. I earned it,
and I'm not ceding to some new guy spewing lice.

Think you can just walk up with a cup and claim your spot.
I know who passes by this corner, and they know me,

know I take my coffee black, don't want a damn sandwich.
I know each concrete pock, each trash can tag, each

wad of gum. Know the ATM across the street
and where the 50-foot line falls. Law of this block

begins with me, what I've earned with twelve-hour days.
Traipse in here all hungry, like your hunger gives you rights.

Ain't give you nothing. We're all hungry out here.

Luck is my myth for blessing

I tell me stories make the night pass
I tell them children in my kidneys my spleen
I tell each fingernail

I always tell me happy movie endings
How lost dog
Come loping home
How mama love her little girl
How we got
Milk and honey and nutmeg

I tell me stories about nutmeg

I tell me stories, wrap my head in scarves
Lucky number rubber bands on my wrist
I tell me little squirrel
He know, he know

I tell me china teacups
So thin they like prayers
I tell me bus tickets and train tickets and airplanes
I tell me places

I tell me blessed
I tell me lucky little children
I tell me stories make the night pass

Each life must have an intermission

Each life must have an intermission; me,
I'm taking mine now. I'm still waiting
for popcorn and candy, for the second half
to start. I reckon I done alright
in the first, got two sons, sold stereos.
But I got fed up with bills, punching in
and punching out, the have-tos, holding my breath
every week for Friday. Now I got

Friday every day, no clock to punch, no boss
breathing down. Punched my way to freedom.
You can keep your Pepco, your Bell South,
your car note and rent money. Me,
I'm waiting for the half time show, girls
with high kicks and shiny clothes, my foam finger.

i, j, k

I wasn't supposed to have favorite breakfast guests, but one of my favorites wore a bouffant wig and huge, clip-on pearls and went by the street name Grandma. We worked to get Grandma disability, and finally housing. Took about a year and a half. Six months in housing later, Grandma turned up again, said the place had too many damn rules. A few months out and a trip to rehab, Grandma went back to housing. I hoped. We hoped.

Junior was the street name of a guy who liked to stop by our office and ask, *When are you gonna get a real job? When are you gonna do some work around here?* Whether he saw me at work or on the street, this was always his greeting. One summer night, I ran into Junior in front of a strip of restaurants and coffee shops on 17th Street. He was panhandling and I walked up and said, *When are you gonna get a real job? When are you gonna do some work around here?* He and I both burst out laughing. Diners and pedestrians looked aghast; one man muttered, *Bitch.*

King, Carey King, was a bike courier and a poet. He often ate breakfast at the kitchen, wrote poems about old men trapped in their houses, the smell of spring, unrequited love. Carey and another bike courier both OD'ed on heroin the same weekend in an unheated group house across from Malcolm X Park. Another outreach worker, who spent his nights scouring alleys to give people blankets, said, *It must have been a good batch.* We laughed like paramedics cracking jokes at the Rorschach patterns made by bloodstains. We laughed because the options dizzied us.

Warm tents we inhabit

Barbecue

We borrowed the incubator from my dad's school,
kept vigil for weeks over two dozen orbs,

carefully calibrating temperature, awaiting movement.
At last, the tremors, fault lines and explosion of yellow fuzz

which made my brother sneeze until the day our collection
of mobile, squawking dandelions was transferred

to the leaning chickenhouse, whose gray, warped walls denied
ever holding paint. It swelled with feathers, feed, sweet smells

of dirt and hay. We worried about neighborhood dogs and foxes,
gathered eggs until the crisp October day the neighbors came,

Mr. Garrell and my dad with axes, Mrs. Garrell and my mom
by a fire and boiling pot. My brother and I caught the flopping,

headless bodies that careened like feathered tumbleweeds,
crashed into peony bushes, hid under forsythia.

One chicken escaped to the woods behind our house. I ran
to my father, begged, *You can't kill her. She's my chicken;*

I love her. I think he was grateful to relent, tell me I could keep her.
I named her Barbecue because I was six and knew barbecue

went with chicken, like peanut butter went with jelly. Barbecue lived
on a rusting TV tray on our front porch, laid perfect eggs, each one

a several-hour labor of circling and settling, delicate clucks giving way
to louder squawks, to speckled jewels I'd hold to catch their warmth.

One day she was gone. I never got another chicken,
but in the store, when no one is looking, I linger by dairy cases,

* * *

open slender cardboard and styrofoam containers.
Finger each inviolate orb, think of hours of clucks and screeches,

routine of circles that birthed each one; long
to hold, to hoard these cartons of once warm hours.

Mantequilla de Maní

On a road trip from San Jose to Manuel Antonio, found
in a dusty pulpería, high shelf, elegant aqua and white label.

More candy than butter, better once stirred, we scooped
fingerfulls onto torn chunks of bread. Declared: Best

Peanut Butter Ever. Found again in the big supermercado
downtown with the coveted orange and white striped bags.

Swaddled in a t-shirt, and two pairs of socks,
presented like an orchid I'd smuggled through customs.

Home, even I scorned the yellowing label, gruel-like consistency,
cloying sweetness. So much of love is context.

The singularly best peanut butter sandwich ever eaten:
on a rafting trip down the Yadkin River, on a tiny island mid-stream,

washed down with warm lemonade, studded with sand like stars.

Somoto, Nicaragua #2

I was grateful it wasn't rainy season, as all sixteen
girls screamed and ran in different directions,

exploding to be swung and held and chased and read to
when over floated little Marijita who hates to wear shoes,

her hair a tangle of leaves and sticks from the mango tree.
The night before at dinner, screaming and scratching to throw

her plate of food on the floor, saying *Mi mamá dice que sí,
My mama says I can*, asserting cook's daughter, not orphan,

plump little legs kicking wildly as I tried
to stop her, saying, *Jamileth is hungry,*

she'll eat your beans if you don't want them.
Marijita looked sideways at the broom in my hands,

smiled as if she finally knew everything,
held out her hands. *Look,* she said, *a little bunny.*

I set down my broom, picked up her little sister,
bounced the child on my hip, staring

into Marijita's open palms, smeared with mud.
I took a deep breath, noticed my scolding

had not made her put on shoes, thought of ringworm,
parasites, scorpions. *It's beautiful; what*

do you call it? Ser, she proffered, skipping off.

The alkalis and nitrates of your sacred offerings

crows turn things blue, bring messages
be careful, learn to watch for offerings

even numbers mean a good day, odds mean watch out
can't listen to pigeons, too many

but if you see an owl, get ready
read your stars in the papers

sparrows always want what you're eating
tell you about the hungers coming

mockingbirds tell you when pride will trip you up
don't trim your beard when anyone's looking

blue jays mean someone's coming and danger
bury nail clippings under bushes near clover

chickadees mean money coming
see gold in their bright bellies

robins got red breasts, mean cover your heart
out here, you got to watch the salts and basics

brother, if you got extra, feed the birds

Life didn't cease to be

There's a point in being drunk
when falling feels
more like righting yourself,

gravity finally kind,
your cheek against the pavement:
the only place it belongs.

Passed out on the sidewalk, pissing
yourself, wet pants clinging to your legs,
people step over or around. I'd step too.

I wouldn't lie. Coming to, I've wondered
if my Weeble days are over. I'm supposed to be
the guy on the game show, winning.

Just a week or two of work and I can
get my tools back. Another week or two, I can
get a place, be inside, bring a girl.

I know, you've heard it all before but this time
is different, and besides my heart
ain't stopped, my lungs keep sucking air.

And I figure that's got to mean something:
Jimmy's hiring and by next week
I'll feel myself righting again, the swing

of the hammer, me holding gravity in my hands.

Where are you going to show your light today?

You have to find your spot. Go to the same spot every day,
every day. Bring something to sit on, make yourself short.
Sit carefully, not too aggressive, not invisible. Be a cherry tree

just popped in bloom, un-miss-able and eyecatching. Smile
a lot. I invent names for the regulars. They make up names
for me, and I answer to all of them.

Ask for something specific. *Fifty cents for the metro?*
Spare $2.25 for a ham and cheese sandwich? Try
for eye contact. Say *God bless you* and *God bless*

America a lot. Have a flag somewhere on your body.
Jack's sign says, *Need money for beer.* Heard he makes $100 a day;
never worked for me. Afternoons earn more

than mornings; November, December earn more than January.
Being by a store helps. *Spare some change*
on your way out? I like a fixed spot, mid-block, but stores are good

if you're making a one-night, not long-term commitment.
Watch out for the over-friendly ones: the ones who want to talk
to you about Jesus, the ones who think you are Jesus. Look clean,

but not too clean. Wear your blanket like a cloak.
Channel misunderstood, but not hopeless. Each passerby
can be your sweet Jesus for a small price.

l, m, n

Lips can tell you a lot. Crack pipes can make nasty burns on the lips, in the center. I kept noticing scabs on lips and thinking fights or falling. When Queen had a nasty scab on her lip, I assumed her boyfriend punched her. My stupidity galls me. If you think about it, it's almost impossible to imagine anyone falling in such a way that they split the center of their lip.

Miriam's Kitchen was the name of the kitchen where I worked. My name is not Miriam, but I answered to it anyway. My mom decided one year to celebrate my birthday at the kitchen. She and my dad came, and I gave her the job of handing out numbers at the door. She brought a giant bag of Dum Dums, and as each person came in, she handed them a lollipop with their number saying, *It's Ruth's birthday today.* Everyone who called me Miriam had no idea who she was talking about.

Nora worked part time at Dean and Deluca and brought us candied lemon peel, praline sauce, and jars of roasted red peppers. One morning she said, *When it snows, I can't sleep, thinking of them all outside.* I tried to tell her having a good breakfast in a friendly place mattered. That it made a difference. *It isn't enough,* she said. The volunteer doing dishes had to leave early so I whispered, *It matters, it matters, it matters,* to the rhythm of the dishwasher, made snowdrifts of suds.

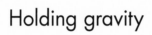

Holding gravity

Over and over I get the idea

Over and over I get the idea to write the poem

> The one about the owl crashing into the minivan after the funeral

>> The one about the piles of childhood toys I threw away:
>> Yellowed doll dress, mildewed stuffed lamb

>>> The images of the cupboards spilling open
>>> Tumble of abandoned cake pans fringed with cat fur

I find drafts and drafts, each time thinking the poem has just arrived

I am both boring and haunted

> Her crying out as I slept fitfully on the sofa
> Cuckoo clock ticking like raindrops

>> I cut her toenails and she was ashamed,
>> Her legs covered with tiny blisters
>> No shoes fitting

To be ill is to surrender to shame

> To grieve is to surrender to a repetition of sorrows

>> Together we die these deaths, again and again and again

In my wallet

Between my driver's license, bank card and three
frequent coffee buyer cards, I carry
the fading strip of four lime-green stickers,

whitening at the edges, each reading, *Packed with pride
by Ruth D.,* to remind me of my two Carolina summers
baking in un-airconditioned warehouses, in jeans

and closed-toed shoes, under corrugated tin roofs, packing
underwear cases for Roses and Zayers, K-Mart and Sears;
of the boxes I stickered and filled, building complex

towers; of the $5 an hour, no benefits that bought limitless
biscuits, used paperbacks and gas; of the chipped orange jacks
for moving pallets, their rust spots making constellations

I named Kierkegaard, Mickey Mouse and Che; of the giant wrapping
machine that spun cellophane around my finished towers,
and the Lucille Ball moments when the assembly line surpassed me;

of the forklift driver with bleached hair who push-started
my perpetually dying Volkswagen beetle, his biceps bulging
like bubblegum, the smoke breaks I envied before I smoked,

the pre-shift wrist warm ups to prevent carpal tunnel,
more like aqua-aerobics in air, slow and hauntingly geriatric;
of the leather pocketbook my shift-mates gave me

my second summer before I went back to college
saying, *Honey, stay in school. We don't want
to see you back here.*

I think I'm getting the Christmas spirit

Blood floods white hair;
old Jack with the mismatched eyes
slumps against the wall. No one knows
the guy who hit him with a pipe. No one knows why.
Jack leans against bricks, growing whiter;
we wait for the ambulance.
I ain't going to no hospital; I want to go to the party.
He is drunk. I can't tell if he has a concussion.

Latex gloves hold ice, smear red
while I hold his hand and ask him questions:
Where are you from? Still got family there?
We talk about the Bay Bridge, anything to keep him waiting.
Sirens flash red and white.
I don't need no damn hospital.
His pores ooze Wild Turkey;
I promise to save him a plate.

The buildings glow with ambulance lights
as Jack is whisked off on their sleigh.
Downstairs, a vanishing tower of ham
a tree now strung with lights and paper chains,
and a barrage of holiday cards
to family members, social workers, inmates and friends
(two addressed to the President and one to the Mayor).
We put stamps on them all.

Inside, I tremble candy canes,
Jack's blood on my white shirt fading to brown.
Dirty sandwich bags filled, like stockings, for later
while Larry presses a ring into my chapped hands,
silver with a wide, milky quartz.
I found it up by the park, he says.
Merry Christmas.

This night will go on for days to come

Cement cold seeps through three layers
of cardboard, two pairs of pants. Wind taunts,
morning recedes: a horizon,

plastic-bag tumbleweed blown just out of reach.
Hands and feet are cold-cracking, less
and less attached, like sputtering crayfish.

I hold out as long as I can. Steam
grates beckon, lure with clouds of sour exhaust,
smell of Greyhound back seats.

Only a sudden inability to believe
in morning can pull me to the grates, iron
filing to magnet. Thawing fingers

negate smell. Enveloped, I am invisible,
neither lawn ornament nor statue. Hidden
by subway plume, I stew inch by inch.

Leaving is hardest. Steam makes
damp towels of clothes, bestows halos
of frozen droplets, twice as cold as before,

morning twice receded. Once you've embraced
this, you can't go far. Must stay close.
Sleep's impossible on scalding metal.

Now doomed to waking, to dance in and out:
Warm to cold. Hidden to seen. Steam to wet.
Held to dropped. This night will last for days.

She yellow teenage whorehouse

She yellow, piss yellow
Yessir yellow when she want her fix

She smile August
Collarbones weights she carry

Street name Lisa
Ain't no name to me

See her high in alleys
See her on her knees

She high summer grass
Sharp and cracking

Tiara fell off, lost below
Eyes purple yellow, swollen shut

She stringless cello
Piecrust crumbling

Screech like Scrawny Tawny lion
Fight with nails and teeth

Gingko leaf falling, falling
Year older every month

She yellow teenage whorehouse
I watch her setting fast

Grip the steeple bravely with your toes

When you have nowhere
you need to be, the hours stretch
and fill with water:
just like in childhood, New Years
is decades from April's rains

The last days are with us, a lost poem

Lord talks to me in blood on pavement;
I have seen hellfire through manholes.
You think there will be time for repentance, time for change,
but I tell you: the last days are with us.
Lord knows I've tried to warn:

yelled my throat raw mid-street at five o'clock crowds, wept
outright for lost souls, on my knees in Georgetown
beat picture windows with my fists, tried anything,
panhandled pennies to copy leaflets I pushed
into cold, disinterested hands, made signs

of salvaged cardboard I've worn round
my neck and propped up when I had errands.
This city has me on my knees and I've tried, I've tried:
bless each passing car with my nodding branch.
No one listens, no one believes.

I'm equally blessed and cursed in knowing
while you walk dogs, board buses, buy stamps;
nothing I do penetrates.
I understand why Tibetan monks become fires—
kerosene is my aftershave.

o, p, q, r

Oscar never sat. Ate his breakfast standing with his back to the wall. Oscar also never spoke. From his age, and his insistence on never having his back turned, I guessed he was a Vietnam vet, like about a third of our breakfast guests. I said good morning to Oscar every day, and after a year and a half, one rainy Thursday, he said good morning back.

Porter was the volunteer who led pancake production on Tuesdays. Porter looked remarkably like Newt Gingrich, and the guys at the kitchen called him Mr. Senator. He'd been coming to the kitchen ever since his daughter came with her church youth group 15 years earlier. Sometimes, to be different, Porter and his crew would make special pancakes – apple, chocolate chip, blueberry. But you always had to divide the batter and make half the pancakes plain. Some people get very upset if you put things in their pancakes.

Queen was her street name. Almost everyone on the streets has a real name and a street name, kind of a CB handle. I always thought that when you don't have much left, you don't want to give out your name. It's the last thing that's truly yours. So almost everyone had a street name. Queen got hers because she acted like she ruled the streets, the parks, the kitchen, the volunteers, and anyone who crossed her path. When she was high or in a pleasant mood, she was expansive and regal in spandex. When she was drunk, she liked to spit at me.

Rumors are thick in soup kitchens. Queen's boyfriend got locked up, and story on the street was he stabbed a guy in the stomach. Junior told me another guy was locked up in John Howard for threatening the president. Frank told me Susan's family had millions of dollars. Donald told me a museum was buying his paintings and he'd be rich. Grandma told me George chopped his first wife to bits. Bob told me Grandma turned tricks to buy vodka. Everybody had a story about everyone else, but my favorites were stories about me. Grandma asked if it was true that our social worker and I (both queer) were getting married because I was having his baby. And Frank asked if it was true that my parents are black and adopted me, and that's why I wanted to work at a soup kitchen.

Day by day, my holes get bigger

brown shirt

Carolina August in our white mini-van, pleather sticking to my thighs, air thick
with salt and humidity, mom proposed a trip to the thrift stores off island.

As a kid I saved all my change for these adventures, lured
by hand-made signs on summer Saturdays. We drove, windows down,

air conditioner on, over the floating bridge, roads glinting with heat.
I babbled of my dog eating banisters, sofas, doors. Mom said her friend Pam

had a mastectomy, that there were special swimsuits now, from LL Bean I think,
with space for a prosthesis, so no one would know. I must have said, *Wow,*

what will they think of next, and let it drop. We hunted on: paperbacks with
yellowed pages, a lopsided dresser with peeling green paint. I fell in love

with a short sleeved shirt in chocolate polyester, cheap guyabera meant
for a guy clutching a sweating beer over a barbeque. She bought

it for me for $1.25. Driving back, she said, *Pam ordered one of those suits.*
In navy blue. It would be the next month before she told me of the lump,

before surgery and chemo. I keep the shirt, which stinks
of sweat and summer and smoke, no matter how many times I wash it,

pinches, a fiddler crab angered by my wading toe. This afternoon comes back still,
when everything changed and I didn't know, salt water swallowed by mistake

when a wave knocks you down, stinging like a new sunburn.

Finding Greenway Esmont on my birthday

I curve up a driveway, and a dog barks enthusiastically.
Freshly painted, newly screened, edged with blossoms,
here, decades ago, my father courted my mother.

The owner is coolly welcoming,
asks if I'd like to walk around the place,
gives me a tour of his gardens.

I want this place to feel familiar,
to see the summer dining room, the porch,
the carport where my dad collected old reed organs,

poor man's piano; ran a classified, *Wanted:*
organ in good shape, amassed a dozen for $10 or less,
tore a few apart to learn how they worked. Never fixed the rest.

The owner walks me around, pointing out improvements;
halfway through he seems wistful, and I want him to like me
so I'm saying, *nice barn, great flowers, beautiful trees.*

The goats all died, he tells me,
one dog died last week.
The horses have bad teeth, are getting thin.

We find a peacock feather;
he explains the females have all died
and the male is well over 20.

Some floodgate has opened: the cats are old
the dog, whose ears I'm scratching, is 10,
Their times will come; part of life, he says.

He walks me back to my car and I write down his address
in case I find old photos of the house to send him.
He says, *We took pictures to leave for the next owners.*

* * *

And he gives me the peacock feather,
iridescent blues, turquoise, purples
looking as improbable in the back seat of my rental car

as my father collecting Wurlitzers
as the very start of falling in love
as summer porch evenings filled with song.

The letters, 1

The first letter arrived near Christmas, forwarded:
recycled angel and childish handwriting wishing me
happy holidays. The note unfailingly polite, like its sender,
a thin man who'd lived at Randall Shelter, wore only suits. I knew
he'd moved to an apartment, thought of his meticulously
trimmed nails, polished loafers. How lonely to leave
even a home you hate, all the particular snores
with which you've shared too many nights.

I thought about a cup and lone spoon I fished
for his kitchen from our donations,
the polyester comforter with blue flowers,
three chipped plates with brown rims. I thought of
the four Christmas mornings he'd spent at our soup kitchen.
I felt a duty, like toward an uncle you may not like
but send cards out of guilt or habit. I wrote back.

The second letter arrived in March, began, *Dear ruth, I am fine,
I have gotten a job as a volunteer at a museum.* Handwriting
so large this one sentence filled almost the entire page.
At the bottom, *I know* concluded the space.
The world seemed full of green and growing, and I felt smug
in my good deed. I turned the paper over. *I know*

you are a lesbian, it read. *Have you
ever tried men? It might
be better for you.* I thought of other ways
his sentence might have ended: *I know
you must miss DC. I know I'll find a paying job. I know
who shot JFK.* I can never learn to expect
the endings I find. I didn't write back.

The third letter arrived almost a year after the first,
near Christmas. I opened it sitting outside,
thinking of circles: new notebooks each September,
ornaments stored on January 6th, the fragile way
neighbors bring cakes to funerals. I hate
my stubbornness and my stupidity, falling
over and over for the myth of the chipped cup,
cakes and solitary spoon, the belief that belief might matter.

The third letter was a grainy Xerox:
a naked woman on her knees, ass in air, head
between another woman's splayed legs.
The woman on her back cupped her own breasts,
tossed back her head, mouth open,
x's scratched where eyes once were.

Of broken folk

Broken glasses, nose scabbed from falling,
I'm the one who calls the mothers
in case anything happens.
he pulled out a scribble-filled calendar
that sprinkled loose tobacco like confetti.
Before his first bottle,

his hands were trembling spiders,
raining coffee down from his cup.
I nodded yes,
in case anything happens.
A vet, he earned the collected numbers
I'm the one who calls the mothers.

of next of kin for neighbors in moldy blankets.
Airborne gave me his mom's number.
His hands quivered like spring;
coffee coated the cracks in his boots.
You remember him?
Got a whole book of numbers here.

A week's stubble smoothing scars,
Airborne died up under the bridge.
Found him wrapped in a blanket.
stringy hair and crusty jeans,
She's up in Connecticut
And I call the mothers:

he said, *It's my job out here.*
I imagined Airborne sailing over the Washington monument.
We got to look out for each other.
I imagined us all, kites released over the Mall
and nodded yes.
I nodded yes.

I learned to be scared at an early age

Some kids got lollipops and nightlights
puppies and footie pajamas;

proud bumper stickers,
lunch boxes, mayonnaise jars

of lightning bugs.
Got candles to blow out,

something green at every meal,
sheets with Luke Skywalker winning;

Good Night Moon,
sixty four colors and a sharpener.

Me, the anti-lollipop kid. Only dark
for me: empty pockets, free lunch,

no candles. But I kept track of how
it shoulda been, cause I *ain't* stupid.

I memorized lollipops
and when I got scared

I unwrapped them in my head,
sucked lime or grape or lime to sleep.

The mundane problems of self preservation are constantly on every mind

Need plastic for rain,
cardboard underneath and on top.
Cardboard like waffles – the thicker the better.

Kramer Books has no-token bathrooms,
libraries, even hotels if you're really clean.
Coffee places throw out sweets at close;

check the alley out back. Find
a place to stash your bags, blankets.
Bushes are good, except when park police

throw your stuff out. If you're gonna shake a cup,
watch out for which corners are taken.
Don't take your shoes off when you sleep

or hide valuables in them.
You ain't a display item;
don't let tourists take your picture.

Find somebody you trust to sleep by you. Carry
some kind of weapon, a screwdriver, a pen knife.
Day labor picks up at 14th & P,

eviction crews hire at the shelters. You'll need
steel-toe boots to work construction.
Ask a church to buy you a pair.

Need an ID for food stamps and clothes.
Need birth certificate and social to get your ID.
Need ID to get your damn birth certificate.

* * *

Place down on 24th is the best breakfast, 9:30 Club
is the best lunch. SOME House has long lines but hot food.
Only give you one pack of sugar. Van comes round

in the evening. Up at Christ House, you can take a shower.
You're out here now. No use being scared.
You can find what you need, if you know where to look.

s, t, u, v

Susan was skittish, bright blue eyes and a fringe of grey hair. She rarely spoke to me, but stayed at night with Frank the junkie. Frank told us she believed her family was pursuing her, with help from the FBI and CIA. Susan and Christine never spoke, but they had a lot in common. After Frank disappeared, Susan did too for a year or two. When someone disappears at a soup kitchen, it is either very good news (they got into treatment, got an apartment, reunited with family) or very bad news (they are locked up, in a hospital, or dead). The morgue routinely brought down snapshots for us to try to identify. When Susan resurfaced, she had a huge scar that almost completely circled her neck and extended up behind one ear, a jagged line of black stitches. The morning she returned, she called me by name for the first time.

Tito was the breakfast guest who followed me in the morning. I walked to work every morning through dark streets. Tito hung out along the routes I walked, and followed me. He liked to bring me presents: little-girl plastic barrettes in red and yellow, tinfoil sculptures, a pink comb.

Urban Plunge is a program for people to spend 48 hours on the street, learning a bit about what it's like to be homeless. Plungers, as they are known on the street, would turn up at breakfast because other people in the parks would tell them to come. They were always in groups, and no matter how shabbily they were dressed, you could pick them out by their shoes.

Vans are ideal for sleeping if there's no room at the city shelters. One winter, a family with three kids and a dog began sleeping in their van in the blocks close to the kitchen. Frank alerted us to their presence, and invited them to come down to breakfast. The wait for space at the emergency family shelter was 94 days when we called on their behalf. A neighbor became concerned and called the cops. The dog was promptly removed to an animal shelter. The family was told to find somewhere else to park their van.

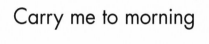

Carry me to morning

W, X, Y, Z

Women and men with exaggerated eyes were the primary subjects
of Donald's portraits, done in craypas or crayon. When he was still
sleeping outside, Donald hid his paintings in the bushes, in trashbags
to protect them from the elements. The Park Service, not known
for their art appreciation, were always cleaning out the bushes and
discarding Donald's work. He often appeared at breakfast ranting
about his stolen masterpieces. Donald liked wine, Boone's Farm, Irish
Rose. One night after too much wine, Donald was hit by a taxi in
Washington Circle. Story on the street is that Donald was dancing in
traffic. After a long rehabilitation, Donald finally got housing. He died
of an aneurysm a year and a half later; I took three buses to get to out
to Maryland to his funeral. Next to his casket were Donald's portraits
of Bette Davis and OJ Simpson sealed in saran wrap. The program
described him as an artist and a poet. Three of the women there were
crying.

X-rays are of great concern when you work with large numbers of
paranoid or psychotic people. I was often told they are used by the
government/FBI/CIA/police/aliens to watch us, gather information.
Some people said x-rays sent them messages, told them what to do.
Christine told me x-rays are sent by the radar dishes on top of tall
buildings, by individual radios which have been rewired by spies, by
cell phones, by fillings in your teeth. George warned you can never be
too careful of x-rays.

Yellow was ubiquitous at the kitchen. The plastic food trays were
yellow. The cereal bowls were yellow. The eggs, the grits, and Porter's
pancakes were all shades of yellow. The canned fruit salad Junior
loved, sliced oranges, and canned peaches all approximate shades
of yellow. Hard living can bring a yellow tint to your eyes; smoking,
coffee turn your teeth yellow. Once you start looking for yellow, it's
everywhere.

Ziploc bags are precious at soup kitchens. Useful for holding: sugar
for later, pastry or scrambled eggs for a snack, half-smoked cigarettes
gathered from ashtrays in front of office buildings, cereal. Keep things

dry in your pockets if you get wet, and keep the eggs from oozing down your legs. Ziploc bags are good for all the things you will carry, and if you are eating breakfast at Miriam's, you will need to carry everything that is yours.

Everything dodges away

My wife, then my job dodged away from me.
Pawnshop for the stereo, VCR. Left

two orange couches, a basketball on the curb. Stayed
on a buddy's couch till he turned me out. Got me

a 5' by 5' storage shed for my amp, boxes
I'd be back for; compressed to a locker at the Greyhound.

They auction your stuff when you can't pay. Carried
a backpack and duffel with books, spare pants, dry socks.

Rolled up sleeping bag, shoes. Someone stole the duffel
when I was sleep. The backpack compressed me

inch by inch. I figured they got books at the library. I
got lighter box by bag by book. Got sick off watery soup

in styrofoam cups. Now, even my body
dodges away from me; I count my ribs instead of sheep.

I'm not like the other ones, dodging delusions. Day by day
my holes get bigger, more and more filled with light.

San Jose, Costa Rica

Doña Mary said, *Come.* Not *Here, help me* or even *Lo siento,*
just *Come,* and led me to her china cabinet. Turned the key,

as I moped like congealed spaghetti on the couch
inconsolable over my wallet, stolen on a crowded bus,

began extracting each glass, each dish, each vase,
handed me, one by one, the fragile objects. We washed

and dried, assembling them like looted treasure, polished
each shelf with graying rags. She lifted a vase, tall and thin

as a prepubescent girl, and told the story of her husband's death
ten years earlier. *Abel.* Her espadrilles shushed across the floor

from sink to cabinet; water sparkled the wedding ring
she still wore. It was long past 2:00 a.m.

when plates were re-stacked, glasses carefully lined,
tiny bells sparkling even the dull overhead light.

Now, I understand this is the purest form of comfort:
not to say *I'm sorry* or *Que lástima,* but to take hands, share tasks,

stand beside, be six-year-olds comparing scabs, lost
in color and texture, hands busy in pressing, picking, telling.

Carolina Clay

Our house leaned and pitched in strong winds. The tin roof
a watering can for black snakes wintering in the attic;

the kitchen ceiling had one-tile-in-from-the-wall painted
for ten years, a racing stripe for our speedy remodeling.

The well water turned brown when it rained; Mom made koolaid
in fruit punch or grape to quell our suspicion. Twenty years later,

when we finally moved, the well was condemned, declared *unfit
for human consumption,* and that was the punch line

to the World's Funniest Joke; we laughed for days. And still,
I remember standing in K-Mart sneakers over the furnace grate

on cold January mornings, smelling rubber adhering to metal,
air billowing up my holly hobby nightgown, making a warm tent

I inhabited; remember the song of approaching rain dancing
tin roof jigs; remember fascination of bouncing ceilings

as someone crossed the upstairs floor. Fringed with peonies
and hydrangeas, sways and leanings made a mansion in maple,

magnolia more alive than any sturdier structure.

The letters, 2

1.

I realize now the final years were different:
you were so quiet, Dad called it *winding down;*

I've been most surprised how he's stepping
toward life, how loves make us moons

to their orbits. It's hard to admit
grief reshapes, enlarges. So here I am

not fully either, shifted. I told you everything;
the end, so deeply silent. This fall is last fall:

changing leaves and amber light. I get angry
people don't remember – I want it to have mattered

to everyone. Beyond deer and hummingbirds:
manatees, zebras, gardenias always in bloom.

2.

He surprised me, saying yes to living.
I wish I could give you these words:

between, lemon, light, fury. I want
to write stories. I will get a lot wrong,

because I never asked. Please forgive me.
When I came for your mastectomy, you sent a card that read:

thank you thank you thank you thank

over and over and over, letters split among words,
wall of text filling the card. There are no words beyond

* * *

I miss you I miss you I miss you I miss

A pint glass from our old mechanic,
filled to brimming with moonlight and loss.

3.

I don't know what forward looks like,
three years both crumb and banquet.

It's supposed to rain the whole time, but I don't care.
I want beach, rain, dog, cold, wet, and then fire.

It's confusing here. Also, enormous cedar trees
furred with moss. Also, moments without rain.

Today I wanted to live in a small town. Today I knew
why you loved small places. I wish I could tell you:

How scared I am. How wonderful things are. How awful.
I wish you would show up with apple cake, give lollipops, say,

It's Ruth's birthday today. Even if it's not. I wish
you could be here, loving me

enough to be ridiculous. Especially that.
Most of all that.

Ecola State Park

Clumps of mosses of unexpected softness, riots of
mushrooms, fist-wide or thread-thin, whole

worlds of dripping. Curving path and then,
broken open: the sky, the sea, our brittle hearts.

Flock of sparrows lifting lightly, silk in breeze,
tiny gelatinous tendrils littering beach,

seafoam blowing: icebergs, then clouds, then
meringue. The dog skitters after sand pipers, foam,

runs circles, lopes toward a dead seal beached,
gaping, rib cage now scaffolding picked bird-clean.

High clean sky and yellow grasses, I am this seal
split open, purplish glimmering; I am this wide sky, clouds

breaking, mirrored in slick sand shimmering; I am this dog
running full out, for sheer joy of wind, for kick of sand,

for rough circles returning again and again
to sea, to foam, to bird, to us.

Take deep breaths
hold a pen
sit still

Oh sky, grant these poets safety: dry socks, lullabies, and soft lighting.
Grant these poets a lifting of insufferable griefs; wrap them

in shawls of spring winds. Bring muses to these poets: panting
harvest moons, fireflies winking beneath wet leaves,

the few brave stars that break city smog.
Cast yourself into gargoyles on office buildings

watch over alleys, doorways, park benches.
Blow soft into each ear during sleep:

You are essential as iodine, precious as infants, magnificent
as twisting live oaks. Send sun to glow within each gut,

shine from fingers and toes. Bless them with wonder for
each improbable dandelion cracking sidewalk. Bless them

with limitless paper and pens that never run dry.
Oh sky, perfect with bruise-colored clouds,

lick each raw wound with sunlight, knit together all that has been torn,
embrace the parts unseen and hidden, and rock these poets

through each long night, murmuring lotuses, blooming mud.

Additional Gratitude This book had a long and winding path to the world, and along that journey I am incredibly lucky to have learned from and been supported by an extraordinary constellation of inspiring people and organizations. First, huge thanks to Peter Money, Harbor Mountain Press, and the MURA Award selection committee for believing in my manuscript and artfully ushering it into the world; I am grateful beyond measure. My deepest and heartfelt thanks for their wise guidance, support, and kindness also to: the ever-inspiring Jana Napoli and the staff and artists of YA/YA in New Orleans, especially Keith Perelli and Maria LoVullo (deeply missed); Kenny Carroll and the writers of WriterCorps DC, especially Nancy Schwalb and Tania Nyman; the breakfast guests, board, staff, and volunteers of Miriam's Kitchen in DC, especially Raina Rose Tagle, Zander Packard, Jonathan Kirkendall, and Steve Badt, and extra gratitude for their work on anthologies to Patrick McGovern and Ashley Phillips; Karen Taggart, the Board of Instigators, and the fearless and world-shaking women of mothertongue; the faculty and my colleagues in the MFA Writing Program at UNC Greensboro, especially Fred Chappell, Stuart Dischell, A. Van Jordan, Porter Shreeve, Tom Christopher, Jillian Weise, and Nina Riggs (doubly deeply missed); the families, board, and staff of New Futures in South King County, WA, especially Tessa Gorman, Susan Lammers, Laura Silverstein, Sarah Schieron, Heidi Schillinger, Susuana Schuarzberg, and Kendra Han; the community, board, staff, and artists of the Clifton Cultural Arts Center in Cincinnati, especially Cindy & Phil Herrick (extra thanks to Cindy for walking the questions with me for 400 miles to reach a field of stars), Barbara Sferra & Herb Robinson, Patrick Borders & Helen Adams, Pat & Andy Olding, Sean Mullaney, Erin Deters, and Missy Miller; the extraordinary team at Seattle Arts & Lectures, especially Sherry Prowda, Mary Igraham, Sumi Hahn, Pam Jolley, Tim Griffith, Andrea Voytko, Melanie Curtice, Lauri Conner, Jenn Pearsall, Rebecca Hoogs, Amanda Carrubba, Leanne Skooglund, Alicia Craven, Christina Gould, Alison Stagner, and Letitia Cain for their inspiring work and support of writers and writing in the world and also my poems; and for generous insight at critical moments, thanks to Christine Sneed, Don Bogen,

Joan Houlihan, Peter Covino, Tree Swenson, and Rick Simonson. Last and most close to my heart, thank you to the fierce and loving tribe who have taught me so much, and have believed in me and my work all along this journey: Anne Dickey & Laura Hartman; Patsy Schober; Susan Schatten; Robin Pachtman; Susan Sanow; Juli Van Brown; Karin Hayes; Sjohnna McCray & Mike Whitfield; Heidi Ob'Bayi; Robin Reagler; Victoria Kaplan; Keiko Koizumi; Michele & Andres Vergara; Kerry & Jay Danner McDonald; Trishala Deb & Ryan Senser; Mike, Laura, Nolan & Alana Walsh Dickey; and Claire (triply tremendously missed) & Michael Dickey.

MURA Award winner Ruth Dickey has spent 25 years working at the intersection of community building, writing, and art. The recipient of a Mayor's Arts Award from Washington DC, and an individual artist grant from the DC Commission and Arts and Humanities, Ruth's poems and essays have been nominated for a Pushcart Prize and won three Larry Neal Writing Awards. She is the author of the chapbook, *Paper Houses, Sky Ceilings* (Pudding House Press 2006), and her work has appeared widely, including in *Alimentum, The Baltimore Review, Cincinnati Review, Ocean State Review, The Potomac Review,* and *Sonora Review.* She lives in Seattle, where she serves as Executive Director of Seattle Arts & Lectures, which brings the best writers and thinkers to Seattle stages and classrooms. A builder and believer in big dreams, Ruth has had the pleasure of leading organizations in Washington, DC; Cincinnati, OH; and Seattle, WA to dramatically expand their community impact. Ruth holds an MFA in poetry from UNC-Greensboro, and a BS in Foreign Service and an MA in Latin American Studies from Georgetown University, and was a 2017 fellow with the National Arts Strategies Chief Executive Program. She is a voracious reader, an ardent fan of dogs and coffee, was a co-founder of mothertongue in DC, and has taught poetry workshops in soup kitchens, drop in centers and the DC Public Schools.